SEE A PLANT GROW!

# WATERMELON

by Charlie W. Sterling



## TABLE OF CONTENTS

tadpole books

# WORDS TO KNOW

flowers

leaves

seed

shoot

stripes

vine

# WATERMELON

This seed is small.
It will grow big.

It grows a shoot.

It is short.

It grows bigger.

**It grows more leaves.**

It grows a vine.

It grows yellow flowers.

It grows a watermelon!

It has stripes.

It grows big!

# LET'S REVIEW!

**A watermelon starts as a seed. It grows in stages. What stage is this?**

# INDEX